SPORTS
DYNASTIES

WAYNE GRETZKY

AND THE EDMONTON OILERS

BY HEATHER RULE

SportsZone

An Imprint of Abdo Publishing
abdopublishing.com

abdopublishing.com

Published by Abdo Publishing, a division of ABDO, PO Box 398166, Minneapolis, Minnesota 55439. Copyright © 2019 by Abdo Consulting Group, Inc. International copyrights reserved in all countries. No part of this book may be reproduced in any form without written permission from the publisher. SportsZone™ is a trademark and logo of Abdo Publishing.

Printed in the United States of America, North Mankato, Minnesota
032018
092018

Cover Photos: David E. Klutho/Sports Illustrated/Getty Images, left; B. Bennett/Bruce Bennett Studios/ Getty Images, right
Interior Photos: Jerry Wachter/Sports Illustrated/Getty Images, 4–5; Doug Griffin/Toronto Star/Getty Images, 7, 9; AP Images, 10, 20–21; Bruce Bennett/Getty Images, 12–13, 14; Dave Buston/The Canadian Press/AP Images, 16, 22; G. Paul Burrett/AP Images, 18; Larry MacDougal/The Canadian Press/AP Images, 24; Larry MacDougal/AP Images, 26; Ryan Remiorz/The Canadian Press/AP Images, 28–29; Fred Jewell/AP Images, 30; B. Bennett/Bruce Bennett Studios/Getty Images, 32; Andy Devlin/National Hockey League/ Getty Images, 35; Ray Giguere/AP Images, 36–37; Reed Saxon/AP Images, 38; Eric Draper/AP Images, 40; Craig Melvin/ National Hockey League/Getty Images, 42

Editor: Patrick Donnelly
Series Designer: Craig Hinton

Library of Congress Control Number: 2017962504

Publisher's Cataloging-in-Publication Data

Names: Rule, Heather, author.
Title: Wayne Gretzky and the Edmonton Oilers / by Heather Rule.
Description: Minneapolis, Minnesota : Abdo Publishing, 2019. | Series: Sports dynasties | Includes online resources and index.
Identifiers: ISBN 9781532114397 (lib.bdg.) | ISBN 9781532154225 (ebook)
Subjects: LCSH: Gretzky, Wayne, 1961-.--Juvenile literature. | Hockey players--Canada--Biography-- Juvenile literature. | Ice hockey--Juvenile literature. | Edmonton Oilers (Hockey team)--Juvenile literature.
Classification: DDC 796.962092 [B]--dc23

TABLE OF
CONTENTS

CHAPTER 1

50 IN 39

It's often said that records are made to be broken. However, some are made to be destroyed. Wayne Gretzky, one of the greatest hockey players of all time, was a record destroyer. His name is written all over the National Hockey League (NHL) record book. One of his most impressive feats came in just his third NHL season with the Edmonton Oilers.

Gretzky was already the youngest player to score 50 goals in a season, a feat he

Wayne Gretzky celebrates a goal against the Washington Capitals in January 1982.

accomplished as a 19-year-old rookie in 1979–80. He scored 51 goals that season and 55 the next. But what he did in 1981–82 defied expectations.

"The Great One" started the season hot, scoring 31 goals in the Oilers' first 30 games. Fans around North America began buzzing about whether Gretzky could become the third player to score 50 goals in 50 games.

Then he picked up the pace, scoring 14 more goals in Edmonton's next eight games. That left him with 45 goals in 38 games. It was clearly just a matter of time. But the way in which Gretzky reached this milestone demonstrated his flair for the spectacular.

5 FOR 50

The Oilers hosted the Philadelphia Flyers on December 30, 1981, in their 39th game of the season. Gretzky got to work right away, scoring on a rebound in the first period for goal No. 46. A few minutes later, he sent a 20-foot slap shot through a pack of players in front of the net. The puck slipped over the shoulder of Flyers goalie Pete Peeters. That was goal No. 47.

Gretzky had a magical night against the Flyers, much to the chagrin of Philadelphia captain Bill Barber, *left.*

In the second period, Gretzky scooped up a loose puck and broke in alone on Peeters. He elevated another slap shot that went in over the goalie's shoulder. Gretzky and his teammates celebrated the hat trick. Meanwhile the crowd began to sense that No. 50 might happen that night.

Early in the third period, Gretzky grabbed the puck at the blue line and skated around a defender. Gretzky fired another slap shot over Peeters's left shoulder for his fourth goal of the game. It was already the fourth time that season that Gretzky had scored four goals in a game. But he'd never scored five goals in an NHL game.

The Flyers trailed 6–5 in the last minute, so they pulled their goaltender to give them an extra skater, hoping to tie the game. But Edmonton gained control of the puck. Glenn Anderson passed it to Gretzky, who outskated a defender and found himself at the Philadelphia blue line facing an open net. His shot was on target with three seconds to spare.

Goal No. 50 sent the crowd into a frenzy. The entire Oilers team surged off the bench to mob Gretzky in the corner. The scoreboard flashed the number 50. A month shy of his 21st birthday, Gretzky had shattered the NHL's hallowed 50-goals-in-50-games benchmark.

Gretzky holds a puck commemorating his unprecedented scoring onslaught to start the 1981–82 season.

JUST GETTING STARTED

Gretzky was a scoring machine that season. He was held without a point in just eight games all season. His 10 hat tricks were one more than Mike Bossy's record-setting total from a year earlier. And he finished the 80-game regular season with 92 goals, 120 assists, and 212 points—all NHL records.

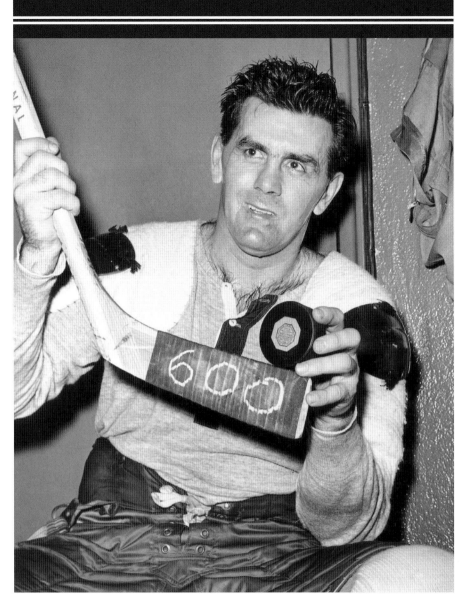

Gretzky was chasing the hallowed 50-in-50 mark first set by Maurice "Rocket" Richard of the Montreal Canadiens in 1944–45.

The previous record for goals in a season was 77, set by Phil Esposito in 1970–71. Gretzky broke his own NHL records for assists and points he'd set a year earlier, with 109 assists and

Scoring 50 goals in 50 games was a cherished feat in the NHL, in part because of the man who did it first. Maurice "Rocket" Richard of the Montreal Canadiens scored 50 goals in 1944–45, back when there were only 50 games in the regular season. He was a beloved star from the NHL's premier team. And for 35 years, he was the only player to hit that mark. Then Mike Bossy of the New York Islanders did it in January 1981. Gretzky shattered the record less than a year later.

164 points. He remains the only player to have reached 200 points in a season, a feat he accomplished four times.

Though Gretzky never topped his mark of 50 goals in 39 games, he still hit the 50-in-50 mark two more times. He needed just 42 games to score 50 goals in 1983–84. And it took him 49 games to do it the next season.

Gretzky's 50-in-39 feat was the highlight of the Oilers' 1981–82 season. They won their division but were upset by the Los Angeles Kings in the first round of the playoffs. But that season set the stage for a decade of dominance for the Oilers, who would bring the Stanley Cup home to Edmonton four times in five years.

CHAPTER 2

BUILDING A MACHINE

A great team often starts with choosing the right players. The Edmonton Oilers had already begun that process by the time they entered the NHL in 1979. Many of their best players ended up in the Hockey Hall of Fame.

Gretzky began his professional career with the Indianapolis Racers of the World Hockey Association (WHA) in 1978. That league began play as a rival to the NHL in 1972, but financial troubles hampered many of its teams.

Gretzky joined the Oilers in the WHA's final season.

From left, **Paul Coffey, Mark Messier, and Gretzky goofed around off the ice, but they were key parts of the Oilers' talented young roster.**

The cash-strapped Racers sold Gretzky to the Oilers just eight games into his rookie year, but even that didn't help—the team went out of business after playing only 25 games that season.

The entire WHA folded at the end of the 1978–79 season. Four of its teams—the Hartford Whalers, the Quebec Nordiques, the Winnipeg Jets, and the Oilers—were granted entry into the NHL. The 18-year-old Gretzky, who posted 110 points in his only WHA season, was ready to take the NHL by storm.

The Oilers added more talent in the draft before their first NHL season. They made defenseman Kevin Lowe their first-round pick. They also added multitalented forward Mark Messier, the swift-skating Glenn Anderson, and tough guy Dave Semenko in that draft.

Defenseman Paul Coffey arrived as the sixth pick in the 1980 draft. He went on to be one of the best skaters ever to play in the NHL. The Oilers also drafted goaltender Andy Moog and forward Jari Kurri that year. Grant Fuhr, who was known for his flashy glove in goal, arrived in 1981. The pieces were in place.

MIRACLE ON MANCHESTER

Everything seemed to favor Edmonton in a first-round series versus the Los Angeles Kings in April 1982. The Smythe Division champions opened the series at home against a team that had barely made the playoffs. They split the first two games in

Edmonton, but the Oilers appeared to take control when the series shifted to Los Angeles.

The Oilers led 5–0 in the third period of Game 3. But the Kings weren't dead yet. Rookie Steve Bozek capped a furious rally, tying the game with five seconds left. Then, just 2:35 into overtime, Kings rookie Daryl Evans sent a slap shot past Fuhr for a 6–5 Kings victory. The "Miracle on Manchester," named for the arena's location on Manchester Boulevard, catapulted the Kings to a shocking five-game upset. The launch of Edmonton's dynasty would have to wait.

CLOSE, BUT NOT QUITE

Edmonton took another huge step forward the next year, becoming the first former WHA team to reach the Stanley Cup Final. The defensive-minded New York Islanders had won three consecutive Stanley Cups when they met the high-flying Oilers to decide the title in May 1983.

The Oilers had outscored their opponents by 41 goals in the first three rounds of the playoffs, an average margin of almost 3.5 goals per game. They had plenty of scoring chances

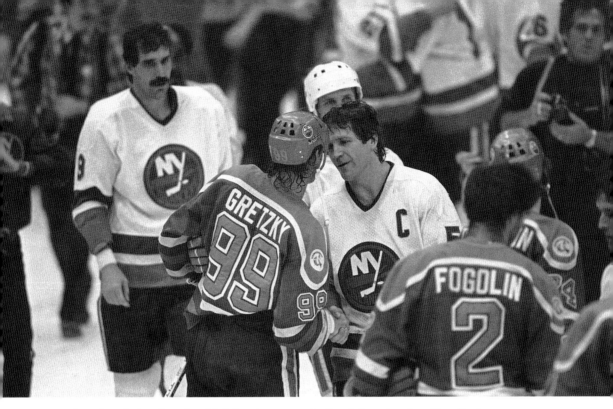

Gretzky shakes hands with Islanders captain Denis Potvin after New York swept the 1983 Stanley Cup Final.

in Game 1 at home against the Islanders, too. They peppered New York goaltender Billy Smith with a flurry of pucks. Gretzky nearly found an opening. Anderson had a quick chance. Lowe hit the post. But nothing reached the back of the net.

The Islanders' defense frustrated the Oilers, stopping their odd-man rushes. Sometimes it takes a lucky bounce to win. The Oilers couldn't find that luck. They lost the opening game 2–0, the first time they'd been shut out in 199 games.

The Montreal Canadiens were at the tail end of a dynasty when the 1981 playoffs rolled around. In the first round they met the Oilers, a team that had won just 29 regular-season games, 16 fewer than the Canadiens had. The experts predicted a short series. They were right—but they got the winning team wrong. Gretzky posted 11 points in the series, capped by a hat trick in Game 3 as the Oilers swept Montreal in three games.

The frustrations for the Oilers continued. They took a 1–0 lead in the next game. Then Gretzky shook loose for a breakaway, but his shot hit the crossbar. The veteran-laden Islanders shut down the Oilers from there. After a 6–3 New York victory in Game 2, the series shifted to Long Island, where the Islanders completed a four-game sweep. Smith was awarded the Conn Smythe Trophy, given to the Most Valuable Player (MVP) of the Stanley Cup Playoffs. He and the New York defense held Edmonton to just six goals in four games as the Islanders won their fourth straight title.

CHAPTER 3

CUP CRAZY

After losing in the 1983 Stanley Cup Final, Gretzky and Kevin Lowe dreaded walking past the Islanders' locker room. Players' families and team staff celebrated the victory, excited about the fourth straight Cup. The Islanders players, however, were in a different mood. Gretzky noticed they looked physically beat up and mentally exhausted after pouring so much into their quest for the Cup.

The Oilers made it back to the Stanley Cup Final with a sweep of the Minnesota North Stars in the 1984 Campbell Conference finals.

An emotional Mark Messier was excited to win the Conn Smythe Trophy as the MVP of the 1984 Stanley Cup playoffs.

"That's how you win championships," Lowe said to Gretzky.

The young Oilers took the lesson to heart. And they had a chance to show what they'd learned when the same teams met the next year in the 1984 Stanley Cup Final. The Oilers had come of age that season. They won the President's Cup, leading the NHL with 119 points, 15 more than the Islanders. They survived a seven-game battle with the Calgary Flames in the division finals. Then they swept the Minnesota North Stars to reach the Final.

Meanwhile the Islanders were back in their fifth straight Stanley Cup Final. But those games began to take their toll on the team's older players. The series opened in New York, and this time the Oilers stole Game 1 with an impressive defensive performance. Grant Fuhr made 34 saves, and Kevin McClelland scored the game's only goal early in the third period as Edmonton held on for a 1–0 victory.

A Clark Gilles hat trick spurred the Islanders to a 6–1 win in Game 2. But when the series moved to Edmonton, the Oilers posted back-to-back 7–2 victories to take control.

Before Game 5 in Edmonton, with the Oilers needing just one more win, Gretzky addressed his teammates. He told them how much this title would mean to them and to all of Edmonton. He explained that all his individual awards would never compare to the thrill of winning the Cup as a team. Then the Oilers went out and put on a show for their fans.

Semenko celebrates an Oilers goal against Billy Smith and the Islanders in the 1984 Stanley Cup Final.

Gretzky scored twice in the first period as they beat the

Islanders 5–2 to capture their first Stanley Cup championship in

just their fifth year in the NHL.

SIMPLY THE BEST

The 1983–84 season is considered one of the best in Oilers history. Their young team was incredibly dominant. Their core players—Gretzky, Lowe, Mark Messier, Jari Kurri, Glenn Anderson, Paul Coffey, and Grant Fuhr—led the way. Messier had a breakout season when he was moved from left wing to center late in the year. He used his physical presence to stifle bigger opponents in the middle of the ice, leaving more room for Gretzky to score goals.

The Oilers set an NHL record by scoring 446 goals that season, averaging 5.6 goals per game. It was one of five seasons during the 1980s in which Edmonton topped 400 goals. No other team in history has done it even once. The 1983–84 Oilers also set NHL records with 736 assists and 1,182 points. And they were the first team with three players to score 50 goals in the same season. Gretzky had 87, five shy of his own NHL record, while Anderson had 54 and Kurri added 52.

KEEPING IT GOING

The Oilers were back in the Stanley Cup Final again the next year, this time facing the Philadelphia Flyers. Early in Game 3,

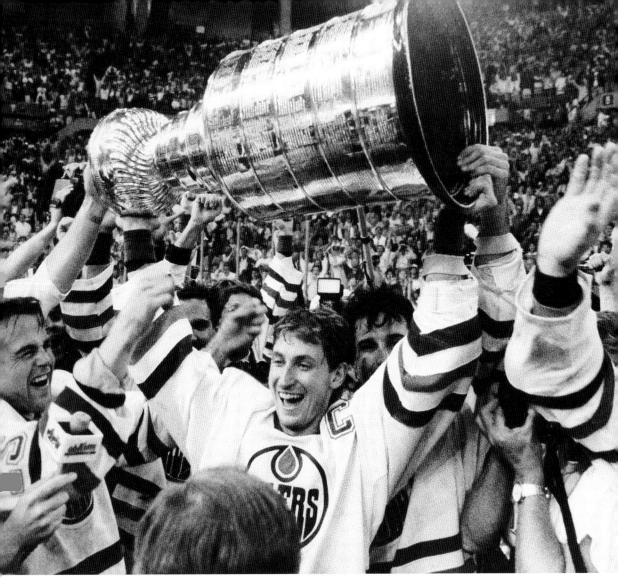

Gretzky hoists the Cup after the Oilers won a tense Game 7 against the Philadelphia Flyers in the 1987 Final.

Gretzky skated in with a loose puck and faked out the goalie for a 1–0 lead. He lit the lamp again 15 seconds later, taking a pass in front of the net and burying the puck. Gretzky completed the

It took the Oilers a little longer than expected to finish off their sweep of the Bruins in the 1988 Final. A power failure at Boston Garden forced the league to postpone Game 4. The Oilers had tied the score 3–3 early in the second period when the electricity went out. The game was moved to Edmonton and restarted from the beginning. It gave the Oilers a chance to clinch another championship on their home ice, which they did with a 6–3 victory at Northlands Coliseum.

hat trick later in the first period. The Oilers won the series in five games for their second straight title.

The next year, the Oilers' hopes of a three-peat went down the drain when they lost a seven-game thriller to the Flames in the second round of the playoffs. But they bounced back to win the Campbell Conference the next year. They met the Flyers again in the Final. This time it took seven games, but the Oilers won their third title in four years.

In 1988, as their star players aged, the Oilers shifted their focus to forming a solid defensive team in front of goaltender Fuhr. The new approach worked. Edmonton faced the Boston Bruins in the Cup Final. Gretzky and the Oilers showed they could win playing any style of hockey and swept the series for their fourth Cup in five years.

CHAPTER 4

SUPPORTING CAST

Gretzky got most of the headlines during the 1980s, but the Oilers wouldn't have been a dynasty without the other members of their core. Mark Messier was one of the best all-around forwards in the NHL for 25 years. He was an immediate fan favorite in Edmonton, where he also grew up and played junior hockey. As a young player, his scoring touch improved quickly. In Messier's first three seasons, his goal totals went from 12 to 23 to 50.

Messier got a chance to captain the Oilers and win another Stanley Cup in 1990.

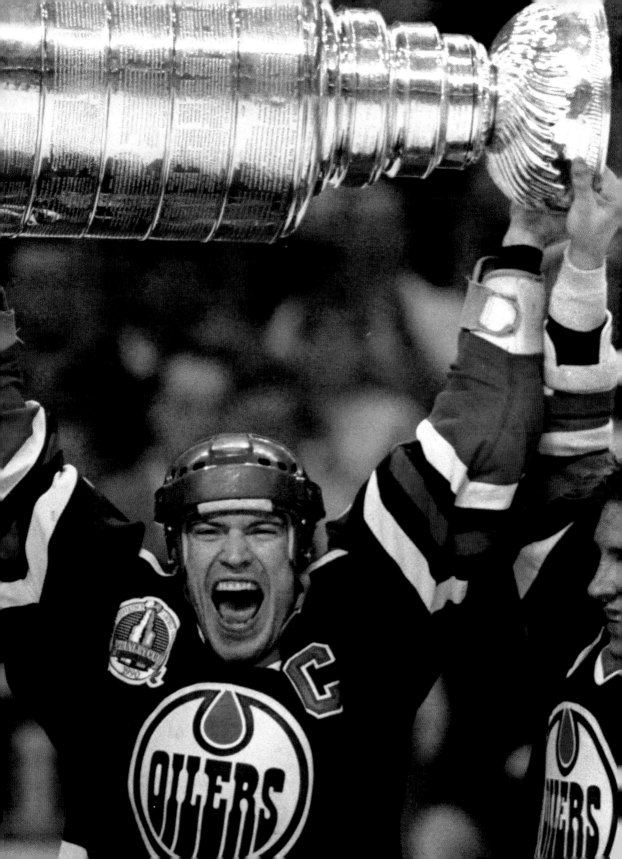

Gretzky, *left*, and Kurri formed one of the NHL's top scoring duos of all time.

The Oilers shocked the world when they traded Gretzky to the Los Angeles Kings in 1988. But Messier took over as captain and in 1990 led the Oilers to a fifth and final Stanley Cup. Then Edmonton traded Messier to the New York Rangers in 1991.

In 1994 he led them to their first Stanley Cup since 1940. Messier was one of the most feared players in hockey history, scoring 694 goals and winning six Stanley Cups along the way.

THE SIDEKICK

Gretzky and Jari Kurri were a dominant goal-scoring duo for the Oilers. They're considered one of the top offensive pairs in history. Kurri starred in Edmonton for a decade, displaying a two-way game with plenty of good defensive skills to add to his playmaking as a talented forward. He made the game look easy with his smooth skating, precise passes, and accurate shots.

Kurri won five Cups with the Oilers. One of his best performances came in Game 2 of the Stanley Cup Final versus Boston in 1990. His hat trick helped the Oilers to a 7–2 victory. He also added two assists for a five-point game, something no one had done in a Final since Toe Blake of the Montreal Canadiens in 1944.

DEFENDING THE ICE

Defenseman Paul Coffey played seven seasons in Edmonton. His lightning speed on the ice was one of his best assets. It made him nearly unstoppable as a defender, and it helped him zoom

Grant Fuhr was a six-time All-Star goalie for the Oilers.

past opponents quickly for scoring chances, too. His best effort
was probably in 1985–86, when he had 90 assists and set an
NHL record for defenseman with 48 goals.

For most of the 1980s, Grant Fuhr held down the fort in goal. The eighth pick in the 1981 NHL draft, Fuhr joined the Oilers as a 19-year-old rookie and quickly made a name for himself. His teammates scored plenty of goals, but Fuhr's quick reflexes, good hands, and competitiveness kept him solid between the pipes. He won the Vezina Trophy as the league's top goalie in 1987–88 with 40 wins, four shutouts, and 2,061 saves.

HOCKEY ENFORCERS

Successful hockey teams typically have good goal scorers and defensemen. In that era, most of them also had players known as enforcers. Their job was to step in to defend their team's star players by checking or fighting opposing players. In the 1980s, the Oilers had one of the best in Marty McSorley.

McSorley stood 6 feet 1 inch tall and weighed 235 pounds. He was known as Gretzky's bodyguard on the ice. If opponents tried to rough up Gretzky, they usually had to answer to McSorley, who had 3,381 career penalty minutes in the NHL. Gretzky so trusted McSorley as a bodyguard that the superstar insisted McSorley be included when he was traded to Los Angeles.

The Oilers retired the numbers of six players from the 1980s dynasty: Anderson (9), Coffey (7), Fuhr (31), Gretzky (99), Kurri (17), and Messier (11). The team also hung a banner in its arena with coach Glen Sather's name and five Stanley Cup trophies.

BEHIND THE BENCH

Glen Sather played a big part in building the Oilers dynasty. He came to Edmonton in 1976 after playing 10 years in the NHL. Oilers management convinced Sather to try a new role, serving as a player-coach for the final 18 games of the 1976–77 season. He became Edmonton's full-time head coach the next season. Sather added the titles of team president and general manager after the Oilers joined the NHL in 1979.

He helped put the teams together through the draft and trades, adding a lot of young, talented players to the Edmonton roster. Sather let them play using their individual strengths, which created a fast-skating, high-scoring powerhouse. Sather's combative personality behind the bench was another part of the Oilers' identity as they turned into a scoring machine unmatched in NHL history.

Another of Sather's top draft picks was Glenn Anderson, a future Hall of Fame player who spent 12 years with the Oilers.

Sather, Messier, Lowe, and owner Peter Pocklington surround Gretzky and the Stanley Cup.

Sather chose Anderson in the fourth round of the 1979 draft.

The winger knew how to beat goaltenders in a variety of ways.

He scored an amazing 198 goals over a four-year span from

1982–83 to 1985–86.

CHAPTER 5

MOVING ON

The Edmonton dynasty with Gretzky came to an abrupt end on August 9, 1988. An emotional Gretzky sat in front of dozens of microphones and reporters. He tried to compose himself. He dabbed at his eyes with a tissue. He took sips of water. He tried to speak again after a couple of minutes, but the task appeared too difficult. The tears kept coming.

Gretzky had a hard time saying goodbye to Edmonton when he was traded to the Los Angeles Kings in 1988.

Some fans blamed the trade on Gretzky's marriage to actress Janet Jones, *left*.

"I'm disappointed about having to leave Edmonton," Gretzky said that day. That was about all he was able to get out as he choked back tears.

Gretzky, fresh off his fourth Stanley Cup win in five years, had been traded to the Los Angeles Kings. The move rocked the NHL. Gretzky, Marty McSorley, and Mike Krushelnyski went to the Kings in the deal. In return the Oilers received two players, three future first-round draft picks, and $15 million. The cash was the key component in the deal. Oilers owner Peter Pocklington said he needed the money to remain competitive with the rest of the league in a market as small as Edmonton.

The trade sparked outrage among Oilers fans who blamed Pocklington. But Gretzky had just married actress Janet Jones and began making his offseason home in Los Angeles. Pocklington didn't think he could convince the superstar to stay in Edmonton when his contract was up, so he made the trade.

GROWTH SPURT

Though people in Edmonton and throughout Canada weren't happy about the trade, it was a big step for the NHL. The league started making headlines in areas that weren't traditional hockey hotbeds. By 1993 the league had added two expansion teams in Florida and another in Southern California. Eventually the NHL put franchises in Texas, Tennessee, and North Carolina as well. The league went from 21 teams in 1990–91 to 31 teams in the 2017–18 season when the Vegas Golden Knights made their NHL debut.

Gretzky scores into an open net against the Vancouver Canucks in 1994 for his record-setting 802nd career goal.

As for the Oilers, their run wasn't quite done. With Mark Messier taking over the leadership role and the rest of the core still together, Edmonton won the Stanley Cup again in 1990, besting the Bruins in five games in the Final.

Meanwhile Gretzky didn't quite produce the amazing numbers in Los Angeles that he had in Edmonton. But he was still one of the best players in the league. He scored 246 goals and added 672 assists during his eight seasons in Los Angeles. And he broke Gordie Howe's career records for goals and points while wearing a Kings uniform.

After a short stint with the St. Louis Blues, Gretzky signed with the New York Rangers in 1996. He was reunited with Messier in New York City. The old friends led the Rangers to the Eastern Conference final the next spring. Gretzky had a hat trick in New York's Game 2 victory at Philadelphia. But that was the Rangers' lone highlight, as they lost the series in five games. The next year, Messier left to play for the Vancouver Canucks.

CALLING IT QUITS

As soon as Gretzky signed with the Rangers, he made it clear that New York was going to be his last stop as a hockey player. He played three seasons with the Rangers, scoring 57 goals and posting 192 points. He announced his retirement in the final week of 1998–99. He played his final game on April 18, 1999, at Madison Square Garden in New York.

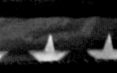

The Oilers retired Gretzky's No. 99 before their season opener the next fall. A month later, he was inducted into the Hockey Hall of Fame after the mandatory three-year waiting period was waived. And the entire NHL retired No. 99 the next season.

After he retired, Gretzky remained involved with the game of hockey. He joined the Arizona Coyotes franchise in 2001, taking on a variety of managerial roles. He also put together the Team Canada rosters for the 2002 Olympic Winter Games in Salt Lake City and the 2004 World Cup of Hockey.

He even tried his hand at coaching, standing behind the Coyotes bench for four seasons starting in 2005, but his teams failed to make the playoffs. In 2016 Gretzky returned to Edmonton to work within the Oilers organization, helping with business and hockey operations. His time in hockey had come full circle. And he might have a hand in creating the next Oilers dynasty.

EDMONTON OILERS

SPAN OF DYNASTY

- 1979–80 through 1987–88

STANLEY CUP TITLES

- 1983–84
- 1984–85
- 1986–87
- 1987–88

KEY RIVALS

Calgary Flames, New York Islanders, Winnipeg Jets

GRETZKY CAREER NHL RECORDS

- 894 goals
- 1,963 assists
- 50 hat tricks
- 73 shorthanded goals
- 122 playoff goals
- 260 playoff assists
- 15 100-point seasons
- 12 straight 40-goal seasons

INDIVIDUAL AWARDS

HART TROPHY (NHL MVP)

- Wayne Gretzky, 8 (1979–80 through 1986–87)

LADY BYNG TROPHY (SPORTSMANSHIP)

- Wayne Gretzky, 1979–80
- Jari Kurri, 1984–85

VEZINA TROPHY (NHL'S BEST GOALTENDER)

- Grant Fuhr, 1987–88

NORRIS TROPHY (NHL'S BEST DEFENSEMAN)

- Paul Coffey, 2 (1984–85 and 1985–86)

CONN SMYTHE TROPHY (PLAYOFFS MVP)

- Mark Messier, 1983–84
- Wayne Gretzky, 2 (1984–85 and 1987–88)

JACK ADAMS AWARD (NHL'S BEST COACH)

- Glen Sather, 1985–86

NOVEMBER 2, 1978

Wayne Gretzky is traded to the Edmonton Oilers of the WHA.

OCTOBER 10, 1979

Gretzky plays his first game for the Oilers in the NHL.

MAY 19, 1984

The Oilers defeat the New York Islanders in five games to win their first Stanley Cup.

MAY 30, 1985

Edmonton polishes off the Philadelphia Flyers in five games to clinch back-to-back Stanley Cups.

MAY 31, 1987

The Oilers pull out a 3–1 victory in Game 7 to beat the Flyers again in the Stanley Cup Final.

MAY 26, 1988

Edmonton wins its fourth Stanley Cup in five years with a sweep of the Boston Bruins.

AUGUST 9, 1988

The Oilers trade Gretzky to the Los Angeles Kings.

MAY 24, 1990

Mark Messier leads the Oilers to their fifth Stanley Cup and their first without Gretzky.

APRIL 18, 1999

Gretzky plays his last NHL game.

OCTOBER 1, 1999

The Oilers retire Gretzky's No. 99 jersey.

GLOSSARY

ASSIST
A pass or shot that sets up a teammate to score a goal.

BENCHMARK
A point of reference against which a goal or achievement can be measured.

BLUE LINE
The line on the ice that establishes the offensive or defensive zone.

DRAFT
A system that allows teams to acquire new players coming into a league.

ENFORCER
A hockey player whose job is to protect his team's stars by using physical play against the opponents.

HAT TRICK
Three goals scored by the same player in one game.

ODD-MAN RUSH
A breakout in which the offense has one more skater involved than the defense has; typically 3-on-2 or 2-on-1.

POINTS
In hockey, a goal or an assist by a player; also a system used in league standings, with a win being worth two points and a tie or a loss in overtime or a shootout worth one point.

SERIES
A set of games between two teams, usually in the playoffs.

SHORTHANDED
Playing with one fewer skater than the opponents due to a penalty.

SLAP SHOT
A hard shot with a long backswing and powerful follow-through.

ONLINE RESOURCES

To learn more about Wayne Gretzky and the Edmonton Oilers, visit abdobooklinks.com. These links are routinely monitored and updated to provide the most current information available.

BOOKS

Butler, Erin. *Edmonton Oilers*. New York: AV2 by Weigl, 2015.

Graves, Will. *The Best Hockey Players of All Time*. Minneapolis, MN: Abdo Publishing, 2015.

Wilner, Barry. *Wayne Gretzky: Hockey's "The Great One."* Minneapolis, MN: Abdo Publishing, 2014.

MORE INFORMATION

INDEX

ABOUT THE AUTHOR

Heather Rule is a writer, sports journalist, and social media coordinator. She has a bachelor's degree in journalism and mass communication from the University of St. Thomas.